Piano

John Kember

Piano Sight-Reading 3

Déchiffrage pour le piano 3
Vom-Blatt-Spiel auf dem Klavier 3

A fresh approach / Nouvelle approche
Eine erfrischend neue Methode

ED 12889
ISMN M-2201-2527-0

www.schott-music.com

Mainz · London · Madrid · New York · Paris · Prague · Tokyo · Toronto
© 2006 Schott Music Ltd, London · Printed in Germany

Acknowledgments
This book would not have been possible without the support and encouragement of colleagues – in particular Gareth Bucket, Andrew Haigh and David Sams. Without their encouragement I would not have had the courage to incorporate the final Styles and Accompaniments sections.

Remerciements
Ce recueil n'aurait pas vu le jour sans le soutien de mes collègues, en particulier Gareth Bucket, Andew Haigh et David Sams. Sans leurs encouragements, je n'aurais pas entrepris d'y insérer les sections finales sur les styles et les accompagnements.

Danksagung
Dieser Band wäre ohne die Unterstützung und die Ermutigung von Kollegen nicht möglich gewesen – besonders von Gareth Bucket, Andrew Haigh und David Sams. Ohne ihr Drängen hätte ich nicht den Mut gehabt über Stile und Begleitungen im letzten Teil zu schreiben.

ED 12889

British Library Cataloguing-in-Publication Data.
A catalogue record for this book is available from the British Library
ISMN M-2201-2527-0

© 2006 Schott Music Ltd, London

French translation: Agnès Ausseur
German translation: Ute Corleis
Cover design and layout by www.adamhaystudio.com
Music setting and page layout by Jackie Leigh
Printed in Germany S&Co.8175

Contents
Sommaire / Inhalt

4

Preface

The importance of sight-reading as an essential skill for pianists of all ages and abilities has been set out in books 1 and 2. Similarly, the principles set out in previous books still apply: the importance of realising the overall style, rhythm and tempo of a piece before you begin to play; the awareness of keys, chord and interval shapes, and overall melodic shape; and the need for a quick visual summary of repeat signs (Da Capo and Dal Segno) and changes in time – an overview of the general 'geography' of the piece.

Book 3 is in four main sections:

1. New Keys.
These begin with major and minor keys with three sharps and flats and progress to keys with four and five sharps and flats; accidentals include the use of double sharps and double flats.

2. Rhythms and times.
Contemporary music often makes use of irregular phrase lengths, unusual time signatures and less traditional tonalities. In this section the less-usual time signatures are explored along with some changes of time within a regular pulse. Pieces with right-hand triplets against left-hand duplets are also included.

3. Styles.
Sight-reading exercises are often conceived to be dull, unmusical and unrealistic 'tests'. In this section the intention is to introduce a more practical aspect to sight-reading and also to inject some 'fun' by offering short pieces to read that are clearly based on works by composers of the past.

4. Accompaniments.
Sooner or later most pianists are called upon to accompany, be it for a choral ensemble, solo performer or in the context of a small instrumental group. This requires not only an awareness of other musicians, but also the observation of an additional line or lines of music. The ability to **listen** and **follow** rather than to take the lead needs to be developed and practised, as does to ability to count when not actively playing. *The value of duet playing is of great assistance in developing the skills of counting and listening.*

An appendix to this section gives a few simple accompaniments which the player may wish to transpose.

To the pupil

This is a book for the student rather than for the teacher. It covers four areas of reading essential to the understanding of the keys, times, styles and accompaniments that a pianist may be called upon to use at short notice. This is achieved by:

a) Furthering the awareness of major and minor keys with three or more sharps and flats (including the use of double sharps and flats).

b) Becoming familiar with pieces in the less commonly-used time signatures and pieces containing time changes.

c) Using familiar styles from past eras to encourage expressive and musical performance in easily-recognised forms.

d) Gaining experience and insight into the art of accompanying with a few very simple examples that can be transposed.

Advice on procedure corresponds with previous books and recognised 'good practice':

> **Always** be careful to observe time and key signatures.
> **Always** consider the rhythm first.
> **Always** aim to maintain continuity and pulse.
> And, above all, **always** attempt to play musically.

The new section, which includes pieces in various familiar styles, will help you gain confidence in identifying the style of the music and the period in which it was written. Call on your experience to give a stylistic, expressive and musical interpretation at all times, and be faithful to the style and performance directions.

Fingering has been deliberately omitted. At this stage you are encouraged to read sufficiently ahead to enable you to anticipate changes in hand position, melodic shape and direction of the music. Similarly, the ability to recognise chord shapes and melodic intervals ahead of playing them is necessary in order to create the correct hand shape before the notes are played. Try to read up to a whole bar ahead.

Reading at sight is an essential 'life' skill for all musicians. It gives you the **independence** to explore **your choice** of music for yourself, drawing material either from the past or from today's popular repertoire.

Be independent: be free to choose, explore and enjoy!

Préface

L'importance de l'aptitude au déchiffrage, essentielle pour les pianistes de tous âges et de tous niveaux, a été évoquée dans les volumes 1 et 2. Les principes primordiaux établis dans ces précédents volumes s'appliquent de même ici : appréhension du style général, des éléments rythmiques et du tempo avant de commencer à jouer, attention portée aux tonalités, aux accords, aux intervalles et au contour mélodique général, repérage visuel rapide des changements de mesure et des signes de reprise (*Da Capo* et *Dal Segno*), de manière à fournir une vue d'ensemble de la « géographie » du morceau.

Le volume 3 se compose de quatre parties principales :

1. Nouvelles tonalités.
Cette partie débute par les tonalités majeures et mineures comportant trois dièses et trois bémols et progresse vers les tonalités comportant quatre et cinq altérations. Les altérations accidentelles s'y étendent aux doubles dièses et doubles bémols.

2. Rythmes et mesures.
La musique contemporaine recourt facilement à des phrases de longueur irrégulière, à des mesures inhabituelles et à des tonalités peu usitées. Dans cette partie sont présentés des mesures peu courantes ainsi que des changements de mesure à l'intérieur d'une pulsation régulière. Certaines pièces contiennent des triolets de main droite contre des duolets de main gauche.

3. Styles.
Les exercices de déchiffrage sont trop souvent conçus comme des « tests » ternes, dépourvus de musicalité et de réalité. Cette partie se propose d'introduire une dimension plus pratique ainsi qu'un côté divertissant au déchiffrage par la lecture à vue de courtes pièces distinctement inspirées d'œuvres de compositeurs du passé.

4. Accompagnement.
A un moment ou à un autre, tout pianiste est sollicité pour accompagner, que ce soit un ensemble choral, un interprète soliste ou un petit ensemble instrumental. Ceci exige une attention aux autres musiciens ainsi que la lecture d'une ou plusieurs autres portées de musique. La capacité d'**écouter** et de **suivre** plutôt que de mener demande à être développée et entraînée de même que celle de compter quand on ne joue pas. *Le jeu en duo favorise grandement les progrès de la battue intérieure et de l'écoute.*

En appendice à cette partie figurent quelques accompagnements simples que l'on pourra transposer.

A l'élève

Ce volume s'adresse plus à l'élève qu'au maître. Il recouvre, selon la répartition suivante, quatre aspects de la lecture à vue essentiels dans la compréhension des tonalités, des mesures, des styles et des accompagnements que tout pianiste peut être appelé à rencontrer sans préavis :

a) Approfondissement de la connaissance des tonalités majeures et mineures comportant trois altérations ou plus (incluant l'utilisation du double dièse et du double bémol).

b) Familiarisation avec les mesures inhabituelles et les changements de mesure.

c) Pratique de styles de différentes époques favorisant une exécution expressive et musicale de formes faciles à reconnaître.

d) Initiation à l'art de l'accompagnement à l'aide de quelques morceaux très simples que l'on pourra transposer.

Les recommandations faites dans les volumes précédents s'appliquent encore ici pour établir une « bonne pratique » :

Toujours repérer les indications de mesure et de tonalité
Toujours envisager le rythme en premier lieu
Toujours s'efforcer de maintenir continuité et pulsation
Toujours, et surtout, jouer avec musicalité

La nouvelle partie comportant des pièces dans divers styles connus vous aidera à identifier avec assurance le style et l'époque dans lesquels fut écrite la musique. Appuyez-vous sur votre propre expérience pour donner à tout moment une interprétation stylée, expressive et musicale et respectez fidèlement les indications de style et d'exécution.

Les doigtés ont été délibérément omis. A ce niveau, vous devez lire suffisamment à l'avance pour anticiper les changements de position de la main, les contours et l'orientation mélodiques de la musique. De même, savoir reconnaître les positions des accords et les intervalles à l'avance permet de prendre la posture correcte de la main avant de jouer les notes. Efforcez-vous de lire une mesure complète à l'avance.

La lecture à vue est essentielle à la « survie » de tout musicien. Elle procure une **indépendance** vous autorisant à explorer par vous-même la musique **de votre choix**, du répertoire passé ou actuel.

L'indépendance donne la liberté de choisir, d'explorer et de se faire plaisir !

Vorwort

Wie wichtig das Vom-Blatt-Spielen als eine grundle-
gende Fähigkeit von Pianisten jeden Alters und jeden
Könnens ist, wurde bereits in den ersten beiden Bänden
dargelegt. Demgemäß gelten auch hier die in den
vorherigen Bänden festgelegten Prinzipien: die
Wichtigkeit, den allgemeinen Stil, den Rhythmus und
das Tempo eines Musikstückes zu erkennen, bevor man
zu spielen beginnt; die Entwicklung eines Bewusstseins
für Tonarten, Akkord- und Intervallformen sowie den
allgemeinen melodischen Verlauf; und die Notwendigkeit einer schnellen, optischen Zusammenfassung
von Taktartenwechseln und Wiederholungszeichen
(Da Capo und Dal Segno) – mit anderen Worten: sich
einen Überblick über die allgemeine ‚Geografie' eines
Musikstückes zu verschaffen.

Band 3 besteht aus vier Hauptteilen:

1. Neue Tonarten.
Dieser Teil beginnt mit Dur- und Molltonarten mit je drei
Kreuz- und B-Vorzeichen und steigert sich allmählich bis
hin zu Tonarten mit fünf Kreuzen und Bs; Vorzeichen
beziehen auch den Gebrauch von Doppelkreuzen und
Doppel-Bs mit ein.

2. Rhythmen und Taktarten.
Bei zeitgenössischer Musik benutzt werden unregel-
mäßige Phrasenlängen, ungewöhnliche Taktarten und
weniger übliche Tonarten verwendet. In diesem Teil
werden weniger gebräuchliche Taktarten zusammen mit
einigen Taktwechseln im Rahmen eines regelmäßigen
Pulsschlages eingeführt. Auch Stücke mit Triolen in der
rechten Hand gegen Zweiergruppen in der linken Hand
gehören dazu.

3. Stile.
Vom-Blatt-Spiel Übungen werden oft als langweilige,
unmusikalische und unrealistische ‚Tests' empfunden.
Ziel dieses Teils ist es daher, einen praktischeren Aspekt
des Blattspiels vorzustellen und auch ein bisschen Spaß
zu vermitteln. Das soll erreicht werden, indem kurze
Stücke zum Lesen angeboten werden, die sich eindeutig
auf Werke von Komponisten aus der Vergangenheit
beziehen.

4. Begleitungen.
Früher oder später werden die meisten Pianisten dazu
aufgefordert, zu begleiten, sei es eine Gesangsgruppe,
einen Solisten, oder zusammen mit einer kleinen
Instrumentalgruppe zu spielen. Das erfordert nicht
nur ein Bewußtsein für die anderen Musiker, sondern
auch das gleichzeitige Lesen einer oder mehrerer
zusätzlicher Stimmen. Die Fähigkeit, **zuzuhören** und
etw. mitzuverfolgen statt anzuführen muss genauso
entwickelt und geübt werden wie die Fähigkeit, selbst
dann zu zählen, wenn man nicht selbst spielt. *Der Wert
des Duettspiels ist bei der Entwicklung des Zählens und
Zuhörens eine sehr große Hilfe.*

Ein Anhang an diesen Teil enthält einige einfache
Begleitungen, die der Spieler vielleicht auch
transponieren möchte.

An den Schüler

Dieses Buch wendet sich eher an den Schüler als an den Lehrer. Es deckt vier Bereiche beim Blattlesen ab, deren Gebrauch von einem Pianisten kurzfristig eingefordert werden könnte. Diese beziehen sich auf das Verständnis von Tonarten, Taktarten, Stilen und Begleitungen. Folgendermaßen wird das erreicht:

a) Durch eine vertiefte Schulung des Bewusstseins für Dur- und Molltonarten mit drei oder mehr Kreuz- und B- Vorzeichen (einschließlich des Gebrauchs von Doppelkreuzen und Doppel-Bs).

b) Durch das Vertrautwerden mit Musikstücken, die in weniger gebräuchlichen Taktarten stehen sowie mit Stücken, die Taktwechsel beinhalten.

c) Durch das Benutzen bekannter Stile aus früheren Stilepochen, um zu einem ausdrucksstarken und musikalischen Spiel bei leicht wiederzuerkennenden Formen zu ermutigen.

d) Durch das Sammeln von Erfahrung sowie einen Einblick in die Kunst des Begleitens mit Hilfe von einigen sehr leichten Beispielen, die auch transponiert werden können.

Der Rat zur Vorgehensweise deckt sich mit den bisher erschienenen Bänden und anerkanntem ‚gutem Üben':

Bestimme **immer** sehr sorgfältig Takt- und Tonarten.
Bedenke **immer** zuerst den Rhythmus.
Setze dir zum Ziel, **immer** die Kontinuität und den Pulsschlag beizubehalten.
Und vor allem anderen: versuche **immer**, musikalisch zu spielen.

Der neue Teil, der Stücke in unterschiedlichen bekannten Stilen beinhaltet, wird dir helfen, Selbstvertrauen beim Bestimmen des Musikstils und der Zeitspanne, in der es geschrieben wurde, zu gewinnen. Nutze deine Erfahrung, um jederzeit eine stilistisch gute, ausdrucksstarke und musikalische Interpretation abzuliefern. Halte dich dabei immer an die Vorgaben zu Stil und Aufführung.

Fingersätze wurden absichtlich weggelassen. Auf dieser Stufe wirst du dazu ermuntert, weit genug vorauszulesen, um Wechsel in der Handhaltung, der melodischen Form und der Musikrichtung vorherzusehen. Genauso wichtig ist es, Akkorde und Intervalle im Melodieverlauf wieder zu erkennen, bevor man sie spielt. Nur so kann man sich auf eine korrekte Handhaltung einstellen, bevor die Noten tatsächlich gespielt werden. Versuche, bis zu einem ganzen Takt im Voraus zu lesen.

Das Vom-Blatt-Spielen ist eine wesentliche ‚Lebens'-Fähigkeit für alle Musiker. Sie bietet dir die **Unabhängigkeit**, deine **Musikauswahl** selbst zu treffen, wobei entweder Material aus der Vergangenheit oder aus heutzutage beliebtem Repertoire herangezogen wird.

Sei unabhängig: fühle dich frei, zu wählen, zu erkunden und zu genießen!

Part 1 – New keys
1ère Partie – Nouvelles tonalités
Teil 1 – Neue Tonarten

1. **Always observe the time signature and style indication** in order to set an appropriate pulse before you begin.

2. **Scan the piece first to observe the overall shape** (this will help prepare suitable fingering as you progress). **Know what key you are in** – major or minor – and always check the key signature before you begin.

3. **Look for additional accidentals**, particularly in minor keys where the melodic minor scale may be employed. Be aware that pieces may modulate.

4. **Read ahead** by as much as a bar if practical.

5. **Be aware of chord shapes.** The recognition of intervals and inversions of triads helps quick and accurate playing.

6. **Keep going!** Avoid stopping to correct a mistake. These can be put right the next time you play.

7. Always attempt to **play musically and expressively**.

1. **Relevez toujours les indications de mesure et de style** de manière à établir la pulsation juste avant de commencer à jouer.

2. **Parcourez le morceau une première fois pour en connaître la forme générale** (Ceci vous aidera à préparer les doigtés appropriés au fur et à mesure de votre progression). **Sachez dans quelle tonalité vous jouez** – majeure ou mineure – vérifiez toujours l'armure de la tonalité avant d'attaquer.

3. **Recherchez les altérations accidentelles**, en particulier dans les tonalités mineures qui peuvent avoir recours à la gamme mineure mélodique. Attention aux modulations.

4. **Lisez à l'avance**, au moins une mesure si possible.

5. **Reconnaissez les positions des accords.** La reconnaissance des intervalles et des renversements d'accords de trois sons favorise un jeu rapide et exact.

6. **Ne vous arrêtez pas !** Evitez de vous interrompre pour corriger une erreur que vous rectifierez la prochaine fois que vous jouerez.

7. Efforcez-vous de jouer avec **musicalité et expression**.

1. **Schaue immer auf die Taktart und die Angabe zum Stil des Stückes**, um einen angemessenen Grundpuls festlegen zu können, bevor du beginnst.

2. **Überfliege das Stück zuerst, um seine allgemeine Form zu erkennen** (das wird dir während des Spielens helfen, den passenden Fingersatz vorzubereiten). **Kenne die Tonart, in der du dich befindest** – Dur oder Moll – und überprüfe immer noch einmal die Tonart, bevor du anfängst.

3. **Halte nach zusätzlichen Vorzeichen im Stück Ausschau**, besonders in Molltonarten, in denen vielleicht die melodische Molltonleiter benutzt wurde. Sei dir darüber im Klaren, dass Musikstücke modulieren können.

4. **Lese voraus** – wenn möglich, bis zu einem Takt.

5. **Mache dir das Aussehen der Akkorde bewusst.** Das Wiedererkennen von Intervallen und Dreiklangsumkehrungen hilft beim schnellen und akkuraten Spielen.

6. **Spiele immer weiter!** Vermeide es, zu unterbrechen, um einen Fehler zu korrigieren. Das kann man beim nächsten Spielen auch noch richtig stellen.

7. Versuche, zu jeder Zeit **musikalisch und ausdrucksvoll zu spielen**.

Part 1 – New keys
1ère Partie – Nouvelles tonalités
Teil 1 – Neue Tonarten

1.

2.

3.

4.

Waltz rall.

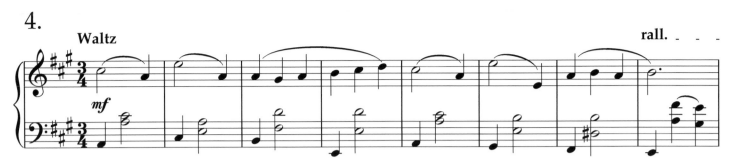

a tempo

5.

March ritmico

6.

Poco lento – in the style of a spiritual
Cantabile – with expression

7.

A gentle waltz tempo

8.

Poco allegro

9. With a lilt

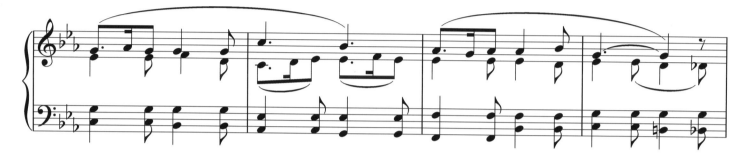

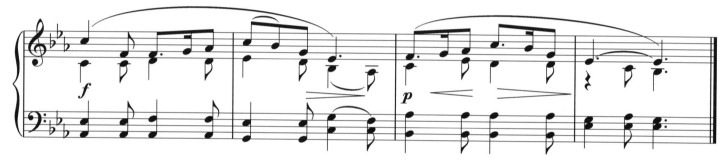

10. Lively

11. **With movement**

12. **Slow and solemn**

13.

With a lilt

14.

In flowing waltz time

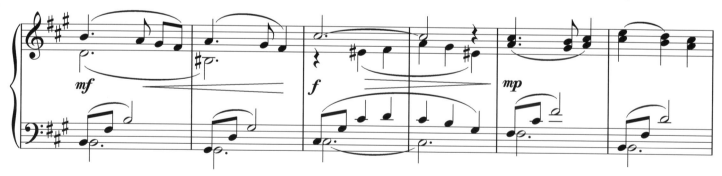

15.

Flowing

16.

Allegretto

17.

Più lento   *sustained and expressive*

18.

Moderate waltz tempo   *cantabile*

19.

Andantino

20.

Allegretto

21.

22.

Gavotte

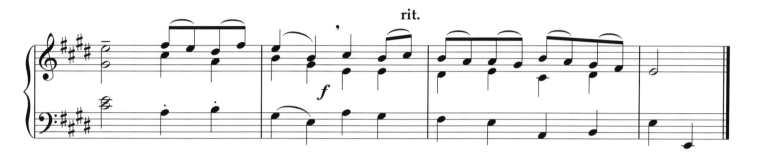

23.

24.

Gently and leisurely

rit. _ _ _ _ _   a tempo

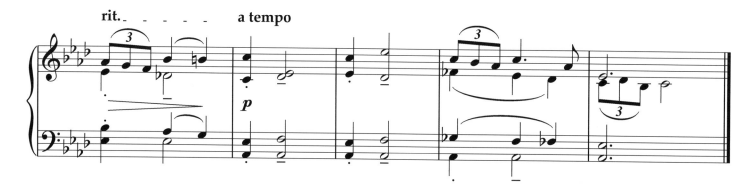

25.

With movement

26.

Poco andante ♩ = 50

27.

22

28.

In flowing waltz time

29.

Slow and solemn

30. Allegro ♩ = 118/124

31. Con moto
cantabile

rit.　a tempo

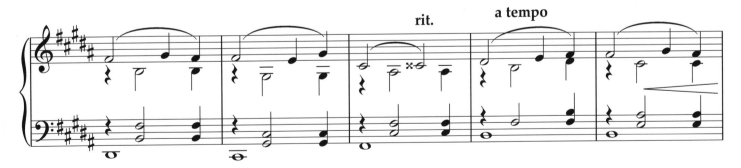

32.

33.

Part 2 – Rhythms and times
2ème Partie – Rythmes et mesures
Teil 2 – Rhythmen und Taktarten

1. Rhythms and times are the main purpose of this section, so **check the time signature first and look at the rhythmic patterns** used.

2. **Scan the piece** to see if and how these rhythmic patterns change, and look also to see if the time signatures change.

3. **Set your tempo** before you begin, taking note of the style indications.

4. Try to **read up to a bar ahead.**

5. **Be aware of chord shapes** and also the use of repetitive shapes and phrases.

6. **Keep going!** Avoid stopping. Small mistakes can be corrected the next time.

7. Always attempt to **play musically and expressively**.

1. Rythmes et mesures forment l'objet principal de cette partie. **Vérifiez en premier lieu l'indication de mesure et observez les motifs rythmiques** utilisés.

2. **Parcourez le morceau** pour repérer quand et comment ces motifs se transforment et si la mesure change.

3. **Etablissez votre tempo** avant de commencer à jouer et observez les indications de style.

4. Efforcez-vous de **lire au moins une mesure à l'avance.**

5. **Repérez les positions des accords** ainsi que la répétition de contours mélodiques et de phrases.

6. **Ne vous arrêtez pas !** Les erreurs pourront être rectifiées lors de votre prochaine exécution.

7. Efforcez-vous de jouer avec **musicalité et expression**.

1. Rhythmen und Taktarten sind der Hauptschwerpunkt dieses Teils. **Präge dir zuerst die Taktart ein und schaue dir die verwendeten rhythmischen Muster ein.**

2. **Überfliege das Stück**, um zu erkennen, ob und wie sich die rhythmischen Muster verändern und vergiss dabei nicht, auch nach Taktartenwechsel Ausschau zu halten.

3. **Lege dein Tempo fest**, bevor du beginnst und berücksichtige dabei den angegebenen Stil des Stückes.

4. Versuche, **bis zu einem Takt im Voraus zu lesen.**

5. **Mache dir das Aussehen der Akkorde bewusst** und ebenso den Gebrauch von sich wiederholenden Formen und Phrasen.

6. **Spiele immer weiter!** Vermeide es, anzuhalten. Kleine Fehler können beim nächsten Mal korrigiert werden.

7. Versuche, zu jeder Zeit **musikalisch und ausdrucksvoll zu spielen**.

26

Part 2 – Rhythms and times
2ème Partie – Rythmes et mesures
Teil 2 – Rhythmen und Taktarten

34.

35.

36.

Cantabile

37.

With movement

38.

With movement

39.

40.

Berceuse

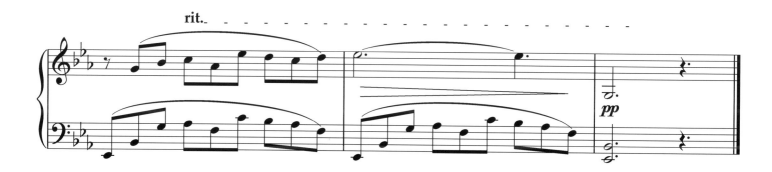

41.

With a lilt

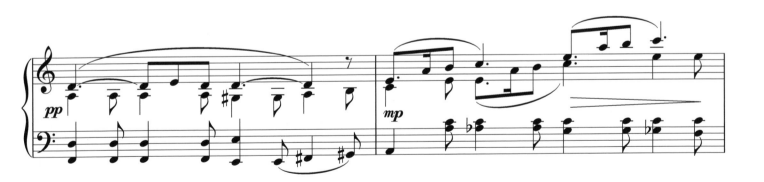

42.

Dolce e legato

43.

Tango

44.

Grazioso

45.

Vivace

Part 3 – Styles
3ème Partie – Styles
Teil 3 – Stile

Although the purpose of this section is mainly for enjoyment, players need to **apply the same approach as in previous sections**, with similar care and caution over pulse, key, accidental and note accuracy. Players (and teachers) may also like to guess the composer – and even the work – that influenced each of these pieces!

Always attempt to **play musically and expressively**. Try to maintain pulse, clarity, tone and balance in accordance with the style.

Bien que cette partie soit principalement orientée par le plaisir de jouer, les instrumentistes doivent y appliquer la **même approche que dans les parties précédentes** et la même attention à la pulsation, la tonalité, l'exactitude des notes et des altérations. Ils essaieront, avec leur maître, de deviner le compositeur et l'œuvre qui inspirèrent chacune de ces pièces !

Efforcez-vous de jouez avec **musicalité et expression** et de maintenir la pulsation, la clarté, la sonorité et l'équilibre appropriés à chaque style.

Obwohl dieser Teil hauptsächlich dem Genuss dient, müssen die Spieler **die gleiche Herangehensweise wie in den vorherigen Teilen wählen,** und zwar mit der gleichen Sorgfalt und Umsicht bezüglich Puls, Tonart, Notentreue und Vorzeichengenauigkeit. Die Spieler (und die Lehrer) wollen vielleicht auch den Komponisten und sogar das Werk erraten, die jedes dieser Musikstücke beeinflussen!

Versuche immer, **musikalisch und ausdrucksvoll** zu spielen. Versuche, Puls, Klarheit, Ton und Balance – in Übereinstimmung mit dem jeweiligen Stil – beizubehalten.

Part 3 – Styles
3ème Partie – Styles
Teil 3 – Stile

Minuetto

46.

Chorale

47.

Moderato

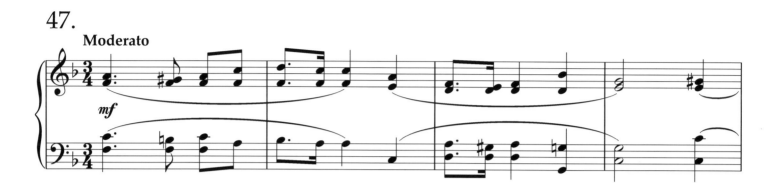

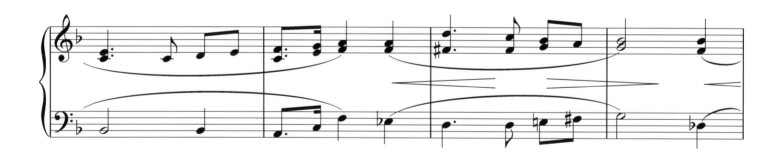

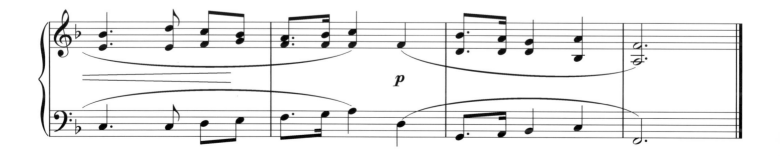

Song and Dance

48.

Prelude

49.

Allegro

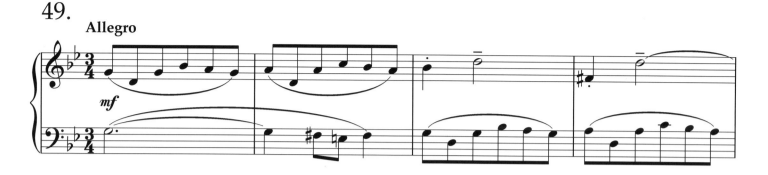

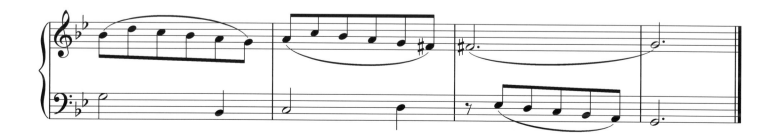

Ground Bass

50.

Allegretto

51.

♪ = 83

Cantabile sostenuto

52.

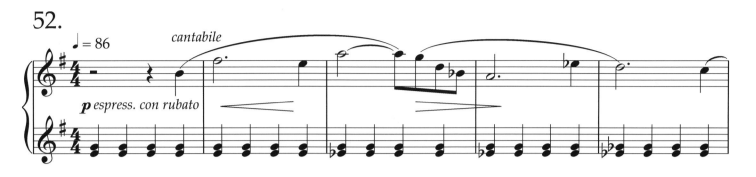

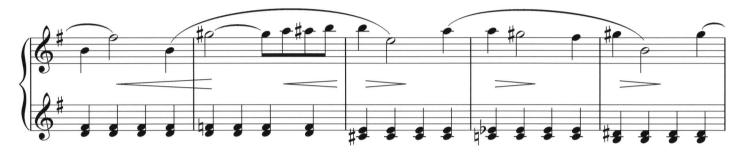

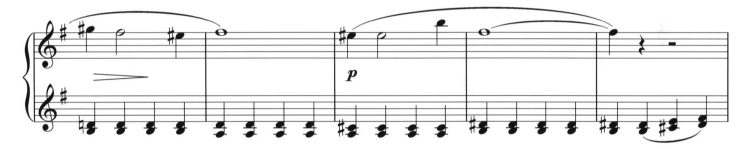

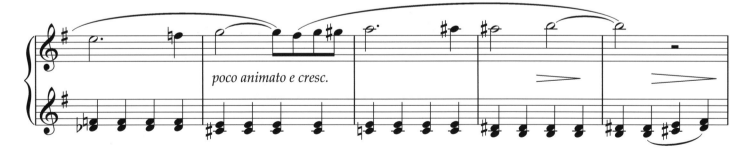

Minuet in G

53.

Pastorale

54.

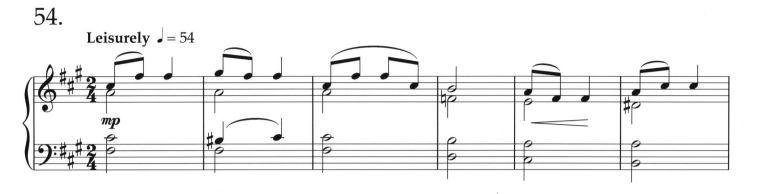

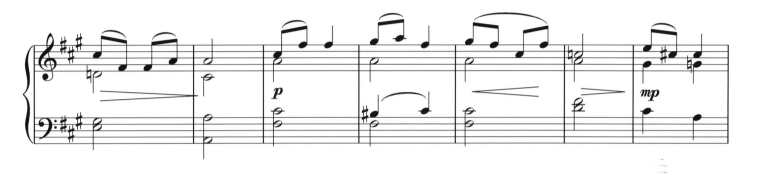

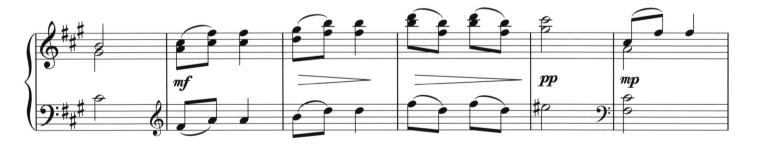

March and Aria

55.

Menuet

56.

Espressivo

Two Hungarian Dances

57.

1

58.

2

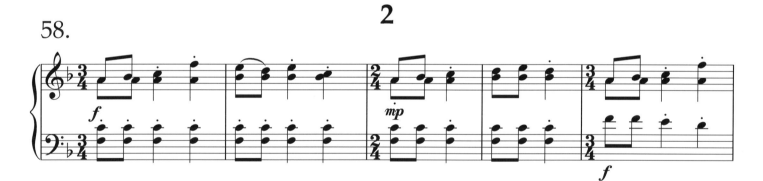

Adagietto

59.

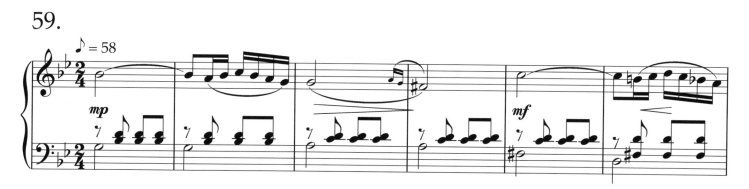

Romance

60.

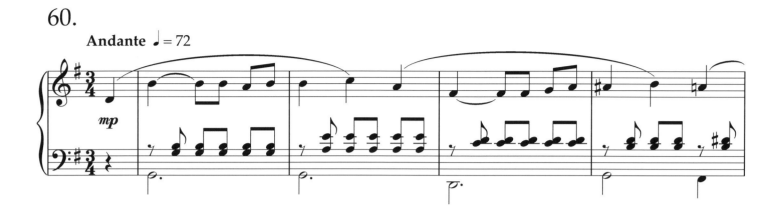

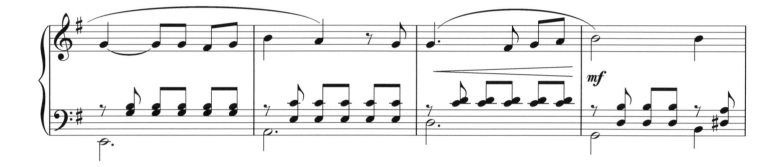

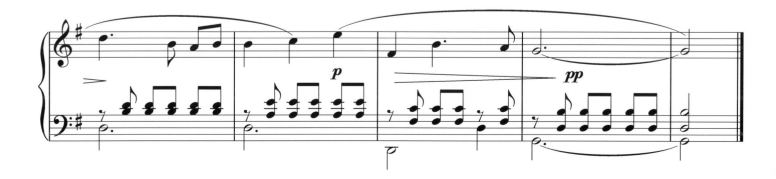

49

Andante cantabile

61.

Nocturne

62.

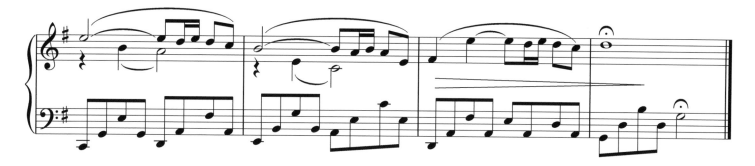

Andante moderato

63.

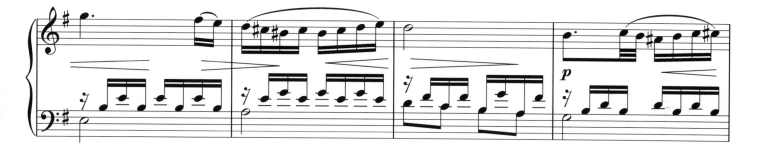

Waltz

64.

Folk Dance

65.

Wiegenlied

66.

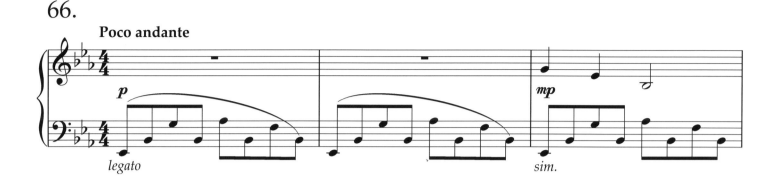

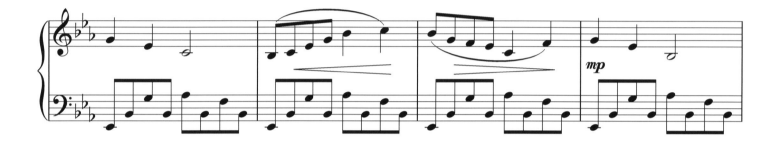

Serenade

67.

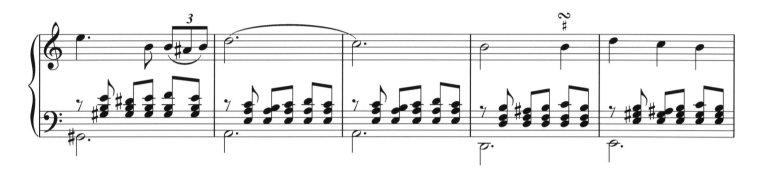

Intermezzo

68.

Adagio

69.

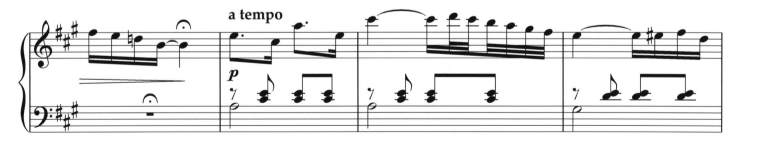

Lied

70.

Andante ♩ = 76
espressivo con rubato

poco animato

rit.

a tempo

Part 4 – Accompaniments and transpositions
4ème Partie – Accompagnements et transposition
Teil 4 – Begleitungen und Transpositionen

Accompanying is often a skill that pianists encounter quite late in their playing and development, yet most pianists are asked to accompany far more often than they are asked to perform as soloists.

Successful accompanying depends to a large extent on an ability to **read chords** and to **recognise chord shapes** quickly, whether in block or arpeggio form. It is vital that the shapes of two- and three-note chords are in the hands before the notes are reached.

Accompanying also involves **counting** and, most importantly, **listening**. As solo pianists we tend to listen only to ourselves and play through an entire piece without a break. In accompanying the observation of rests and the need for counting becomes more important, as it is essential to follow the pulse and variations in expression of the soloist.

Examples here are given in a few of the more common accompanying styles and also in others that are perhaps less familiar; this is to encourage both counting and following a varying tempo. Teachers may wish to imitate a soloist with a poor sense of pulse or an exaggerated sense of rubato in order to encourage the accompanist to **follow rather than lead**. It is also a good idea to make use of readily available simple accompaniments, which can be found in the easier pieces for (non-transposing) instruments such as flute and violin.

L'**accompagnement** est parfois un aspect de leur activité que les pianistes n'abordent que tard dans leurs parcours, bien qu'ils soient beaucoup plus souvent sollicités pour accompagner que pour jouer en soliste.

Un accompagnement réussi s'appuie largement sur la capacité de **lire les accords** et de **reconnaître** rapidement **leurs positions**, qu'ils soient plaqués ou arpégés. Il est essentiel que les mains anticipent la posture requise par les accords de deux ou trois notes avant d'atteindre les touches.

L'accompagnement suppose également une aptitude à **compter** et, surtout, à **écouter**. Le pianiste, habitué à jouer en soliste, a tendance à n'écouter que lui-même et à jouer sans s'interrompre. En tant qu'accompagnateur, il lui devient nécessaire d'observer scrupuleusement les silences et de compter avec rigueur, de même qu'il lui est indispensable de suivre la pulsation établie par le soliste et ses variantes expressives.

Les exemples d'accompagnements proposés ici, dans quelques-uns des styles d'accompagnements les plus couramment rencontrés et dans d'autres moins familiers, sont destinés à habituer le pianiste au respect de la battue tout en suivant un *tempo* plus ou moins régulier. Les professeurs pourront imiter le jeu d'un soliste au sens de la pulsation peu fiable ou à la tendance exagérée au *rubato* pour entraîner l'accompagnateur à **suivre plutôt qu'à mener**. On pourra également se servir avec profit des accompagnements simples fournis avec les pièces faciles pour des instruments (non-transpositeurs) tels que flûte et violon.

Das **Begleiten** ist eine Fähigkeit, die Pianisten oft recht spät in ihrer Spielerlaufbahn und Entwicklung erwerben, obwohl die meisten viel häufiger gebeten werden zu begleiten anstatt als Solist aufzutreten.

Erfolgreiches Begleiten hängt zu einem großen Ausmaß von der Fähigkeit ab, **Akkorde lesen** und **Akkordformen** schnell **wieder erkennen zu können**, ob das nun in Block- oder Arpeggioform ist. Es ist unerlässlich, dass man weiß, wie die verschiedenen Formen der 2er- und 3er-Akkorde gegriffen werden, bevor man die entsprechenden Noten erreicht.

Begleiten beinhaltet ebenso **Zählen** und, am allerwichtigsten, **Zuhören**. Als Solist neigen wir dazu, nur uns selbst zuzuhören und ein ganzes Stück ohne Pause durchzuspielen. Beim Begleiten bekommt das Einhalten von Pausen und die Notwendigkeit des Zählens eine größere Bedeutung, da es unbedingt erforderlich ist, den Puls durchzuhalten und den Ausdrucksvarianten des Solisten zu folgen.

Die Beispiele hier decken sowohl einige bekanntere Begleitstile ab als auch einige, die vielleicht nicht so geläufig sind; sie sollen dazu ermutigen, sowohl zu zählen als auch sich ändernden Geschwindigkeiten anzupassen. Lehrer könnten vielleicht einen Solisten imitieren, der einen miserablen Sinn für den Pulsschlag oder einen übertriebenen Hang zum Rubato hat, um den Begleiter dazu zu bringen, **zu folgen statt zu führen**. Eine weitere gute Idee ist es, leicht zugängliche einfache Begleitungen zu nutzen, die in den einfacheren Stücken für (nicht transponierende) Instrumente, wie z. B. Flöte oder Geige, zu finden sind.

60

Transposition

Transposition at the piano is conceived by many to be an advanced skill beyond the needs of ordinary pianists. With a little application, however, it may prove to be not as difficult as at first thought.

- **Think of the new key.** Know which accidentals will change and know the main dominant and tonic chords in the new key.

- **Follow the shape and intervals in the melody**, and notice the chord shapes.

- Constantly think of the new key – **don't just concentrate on the start.**

- It is generally agreed that it is **easier to transpose down than up**, so try that first.

- Pianist may like to develop this skill by **beginning with simple right-hand and left-hand melodies**, like those found in Book 1, and later moving on to simple hands-together pieces, such as those found at the start of Book 2.

Transposition

La transposition au piano est considérée par beaucoup comme une capacité avancée dépassant les besoins habituels des pianistes. Toutefois, avec un minimum d'application, cette démarche se révélera peut-être moins complexe qu'il n'y paraît.

- **Réfléchissez à la nouvelle tonalité**, aux altérations qui vont changer et repérez les accords de dominante et de tonique de la nouvelle tonalité.

- **Suivez les contours de la mélodie et les intervalles qui y sont con-tenus** et observez les positions des accords.

- Concentrez-vous sans cesse sur la nouvelle tonalité – et **pas uniquement sur le début du morceau.**

- De l'avis général, il est **plus facile de transposer vers le grave** que vers l'**aigu**. Entraînez-vous d'abord à la transposition inférieure.

- Commencez par transposer des **mélodies simples mains sé parées**, comme celles proposées par le volume 1, puis attaquez-vous à des pièces faciles **mains ensemble**, comme celles proposées au début du volume 2.

Transpositionen

Transpositionen auf dem Klavier werden von vielen als eine fortgeschrittene Fähigkeit betrachtet, die über das Handwerkszeug für einen normalen Pianisten hinausgeht. Mit ein bisschen Anleitung allerdings erweisen sie sich vielleicht als nicht so schwierig, wie man anfänglich dachte.

- **Konzentriere dich auf die neue Tonart.** Habe die Vorzeichen, die sich ändern, im Kopf und kenne die Hauptakkorde der Dominanten und Tonika in der neuen Tonart.

- **Folge den Formen und Inter vallen in der Melodie**, und verinnerliche die Akkordformen.

- Denke ständig an die neue Tonart – **konzentriere dich nicht nur auf den Anfang.**

- Ganz allgemein geht man davon aus, dass es **einfacher ist, aufwärts als abwärts zu transponieren** – versuche das daher zuerst.

- Eine gute Möglichkeit für den Pianisten, diese Fähigkeit zu entwickeln, ist es, **mit leichten Melodien für die rechte und linke Hand zu beginnen**, wie man sie im ersten Band findet. Später geht man dann zu leichten Stücken für beide Hände über, wie sie zu Beginn des zweiten Bandes stehen.

Part 4 – Accompaniments and transpositions
4ème Partie – Accompagnements et transposition
Teil 4 – Begleitungen und Transpositionen

Accompaniments.   Accompagnements.   Begleitungen.

71.

72.

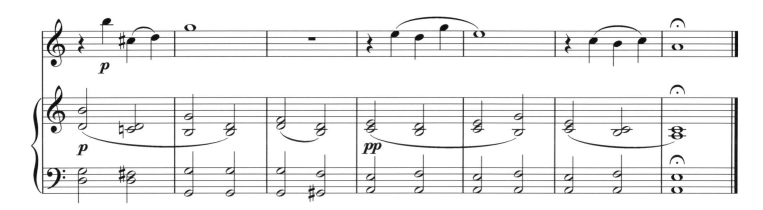

73.

74.

Poco lento e rubato

75.

76.

With a lilt

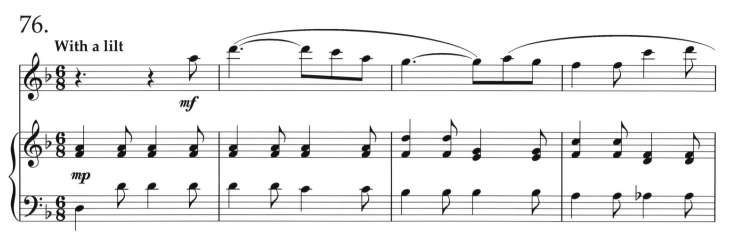

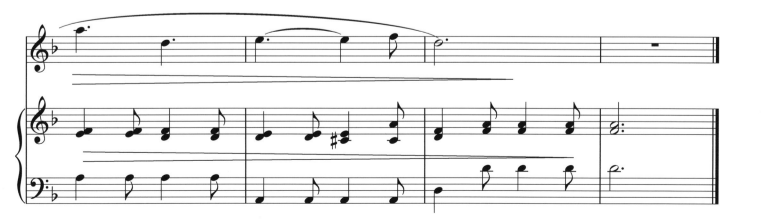

77.

Con moto

78.

Quick waltz ♩ = c.130

79.

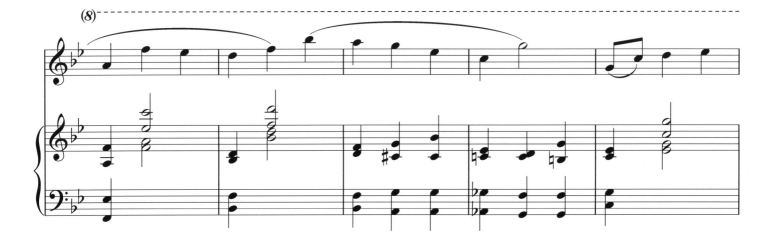

80.

Dreamily – in free time

81.

82.

Allegro

83. Moderato

84. Giocoso

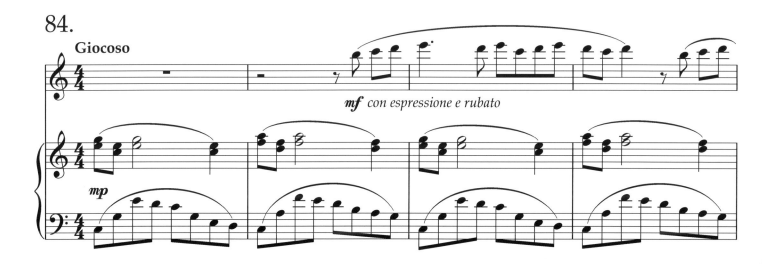

mf con espressione e rubato

con Ped.

85.

Transpose this down a tone into
F major.

A transposer un ton en dessous en
fa majeur.

Transponiere dieses Stück einen
Ton tiefer nach F-Dur.

86.

Transpose this down a tone into
C major.

A transposer un ton en dessous en
do majeur.

Transponiere dieses Stück einen
Ton tiefer nach C-Dur.

87.

76

Transpose this down a tone into D minor.

A transposer un ton en dessous en *ré* mineur.

Transponiere dieses Stück einen Ton tiefer nach d-Moll.

88.

Transpose this down a tone into Bᵇ major.

A transposer un ton en dessous en *si*ᵇ majeur.

Transponiere dieses Stück einen Ton tiefer nach B-Dur.

89.

| Transpose this down a tone into A♭ major and up a tone into C major. | A transposer un ton en dessous en *la♭* majeur et un ton au-dessus en *do* majeur. | Transponiere dieses Stück einen Ton tiefer nach As-Dur und einen Ton höher nach C-Dur. |

90.

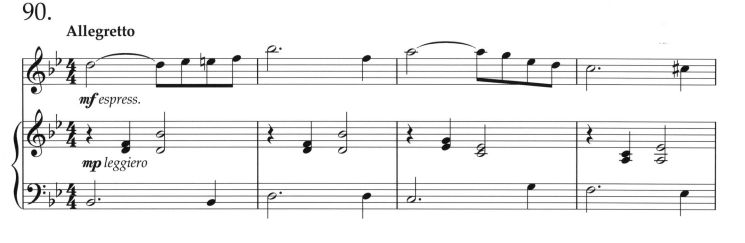

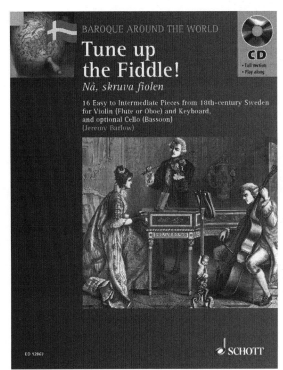

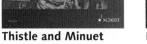